The 32 Worst Mistakes People Make About Dogs

AMY LAURENS

OTHER WORKS
Find other works by the author at
http://www.amylaurens.com/books/

The 32 Worst Mistakes People Make About Dogs

AMY LAURENS

Inkprint PRESS
www.inkprintpress.com

Copyright © 2017 Amy Laurens

Large portions of this text first appeared under the title *The 33 Worst Mistakes Writers Make About Dogs,* first edition published in 2009 by One More Word, second edition digitally published in 2012 by ACOA, first published in paperback by Inkprint Press in 2014.

2 4 6 8 10 9 7 5 3 1

All rights reserved. No part of this book may be reproduced in any form or by any electronic or mechanical means, including information storage and retrieval systems, without permission in writing from the publisher, except by a reviewer, who may quote brief passages in a review.

Legal disclaimer: The information in this book is intended as general advice only. Always consult an expert.

ISBN: 978-1-925825-92-3

National Library of Australia Cataloguing-in-Publication Data
Laurens, Amy 1985—
The 32 Worst Mistakes People Make About Dogs
Includes bibliographical references. 101 p.
ISBN: 978-1-925825-92-3
Inkprint Press, Canberra, Australia

1. Dogs 2. Dogs—Psychology 3. Dogs—Anecdotes 4. Dogs—Behaviour

Printed in Australia.

Cover images and design © Amy Laurens.

For Chloe, Mindy, Abbi, Laura and Max, and all the other dogs who have made a difference in somebody's life.

CONTENTS

Acknowledgments	i
Introduction	1
Section One: People in Fur Coats	3
Section Two: The Senses	19
Section Three: Learning and Development	34
Section Four: Communication	53
Section Five: Pedigrees and Breeding	64
Conclusion	83
References	85

ACKNOWLEDGMENTS

Thanks to Maigen Turner for letting me use some of her stories. To Liana Brooks for reassurance through many drafts, both of this book and many others, and for being the one who makes me keep writing on the bad days. To Ada Hoffmann for help getting the science right (the remaining errors are, of course, all mine). And finally, thanks to Daimien, for telling me I could do it.

INTRODUCTION

Brothers and sisters, I bid you beware,
Of giving your heart to a dog to tear.

~Rudyard Kipling

It's a funny thing, writing a book about dogs. A huge percentage of the population has owned or currently owns a dog, and it seems that as with children, everyone who has a dog knows the best way to raise them. As a culture, we are pretty dog-savvy, and the dog's position as man's best friend is well established in our arts and entertainment.

You might think, then, that a book on mistakes that people make about dogs would be a slim volume indeed. In actual fact, the opposite is true. Many of the mistakes that people make about dogs are made not because people know nothing about dogs, but because so much of the cultural knowledge we possess is false. Myths about animals abound, and it seems the more important the animal is to humanity, the more myths it will generate.

So what makes my perspective worthwhile? First of all, I've dealt with a wide variety of dogs in a wide variety of situations ever since I was little. I won my first obedience ribbon with a dog at age twelve, and saw puppies born in my own backyard when I was seven—and the very first puppy I bred myself became an Australian Champion at 14 months of age.

I've done obedience trials and conformation showing, and started training dogs as all-purpose house assistants;

I'm a registered Labrador Retriever breeder and have experienced the joys and woes of breeding and raising our own litters, and consequently the deep bond that develops when you own a dog from birth.

I've hit the training paddock in the deep, miserable wet of winter, and I've suffered through the consequences of no-dog-walks-for-a-month. If there's a mistake to be made, I'm pretty sure by now that I've made it, and kicked myself in the rear end about it later.

I've seen people suffer from making the same mistakes over and over again, and in writing this book I want to offer you the opportunity to learn from my mistakes—to be a dog-savvy citizen who gets it right.

I want to answer some of the questions that people who have grown up around dogs and people who have never had a dog both forget to ask.

This book is divided into six core sections:

People In Fur Coats, which establishes a baseline for interpreting and understanding canine behaviour;

The Senses, which explores the various ways in which dogs receive information from their surroundings;

Learning and Development, which delves into the way in which dogs learn;

Communication, the section which contains perhaps the most common of all mistakes;

Pedigrees and Breeding, which deals with common misconceptions about breeds, mongrels, and their associated bad habits; and finally,

Relationships, discussing the various complexities that come with meshing the personality of a dog with that of a person.

I hope you enjoy it, and find it useful.

SECTION ONE: PEOPLE IN FUR COATS

In modern, westernised society, the assumed calling of the vast majority of dogs is 'companion'. Dogs feature in our lives because we or people we know keep them as pets, and although occasionally people might move beyond companionship to exploring other things dogs are capable of, for the most part that's the extent of our relationship.

Sadly, this leads to some of the most significant mistakes people make concerning dogs. We assume that because they are our companions—and because they seem to enjoy our companionship—that they are simply humans in a different form; people, if you will, in fur coats. But dogs are not people. They experience the world in different ways, and they process it differently, too. They are their own unique species, and to understand them as anything less is to do them a gross disservice.

MISTAKE 1: WE'RE ALL IN THIS TOGETHER

Even though dogs are decidedly non-human and have their own way of experiencing the world, it's good to have a baseline understanding of the way in which we are the same—we *are* all mammals, and mammal brains share the fundamentals in terms of how we're wired.

Mammal brains have four primary differences to the brains of other animals.

1) Mammal brains are much larger, comparative to body weight;

2) the hippocampus, responsible for spatial memory, navigation and the conversion of short to long term memory, is larger and more developed;

3) the amygdala is also more developed, taking on the additional role of processing and remembering emotions; and

4) mammal brains have a neocortex, responsible for processing a lot of our sensory information as well as dealing with our working memory and social and emotional processing.

It's easy to see what the key features are here: in general terms, mammals have better memories than non-mammals, as well as the ability to remember and process emotions.

This makes us pretty social beings, something that we know instinctively—dogs form packs, horses form herds, and even usually-solitary animals like tigers have a set of social rules more complex than your average lizard or fish (though these too do have social rules!).

And besides—dogs are just plain snugglier than birds.

- Dogs are not totally alien; they have the same basic brain chemistry as humans.
- Because of this, the foundation for their experience of life is similar to ours: they remember things, they learn, and they are social.

MISTAKE 2: EMOTION

I don't have the space—and nor is it the purpose of this book—to get into the nitty-gritty of what exactly emotion *is*. If, however, you are so inclined, there is a wonderful discussion of exactly this in the first chapter of Patricia McConnell's *For The Love Of A Dog*.

Pretty much everyone who has ever owned a dog agrees instinctively that dogs must have at least *some* sense of emotion, and the fact that mammals share the parts of the brain responsible for dealing with emotion is weighty evidence in favor of the idea that dogs experience emotion.

In fact, even though some scientists are still reluctant to come right out and attribute emotion to animals, there is a growing body of evidence to suggest that not only might dogs experience basic emotions, their emotional experiences may actually be closer to those of human than any other non-human creature, including primates.

Evidence suggests that dogs can experience emotions like fear, affection, contentedness and discomfort (which are, less precisely, happiness and sadness). In very general terms, I think what makes these emotions different to more complex emotions is that they are essentially response-to-stimuli feelings. You don't need an understanding of the social dynamics involved in a situation to feel comfortable or uncomfortable, scared or affectionate (although social interactions can cause these feelings too).

In contrast, it's hard to feel guilty about something unless you have a sense of what you were *supposed* to do, which involves an understanding of the social norms required in a situation. The same applies to feelings like embarrassment or regret. A dog's frontal cortex (responsible for recognizing future consequences, planning, inhibition and perceiving difference/similarity) is not as highly developed as that of humans, and their social norms are different.

People are often convinced that their dog is feeling guilty or embarrassed. However, most of what we interpret as a dog 'looking guilty' is actually the dog attempting to look submissive, because it can read in our body language (or from past experience) that punishment is coming; it's not so much 'I know I did something wrong, I'm sorry, please forgive me' as 'You look upset, but I'm small, and submissive, and will keep out of your way, so please don't take it out on me'.

Likewise, dogs are not capable of plotting revenge. My dogs are well house-broken, and Laura will actually ring a bell on the door to let us know that she needs to go out. However, even she has peed on the carpet once when we were out, not to 'get back at us' for locking her in the house and daring to go out, but because she couldn't hold it any longer. She did something she'd been trained to avoid because her need (which can often be a reaction to fear, though not in this instance) was stronger than her training.

- It's very likely that dogs experience basic emotions like fear, affection, happiness and loneliness.
- However, because their frontal cortex is not as

developed as that of humans, and because their social norms are very different, it's unlikely that they experience more complex emotions like regret, guilt, revenge, and embarrassment, as least as we understand these feelings.

MISTAKE 3: DOGS GET GRUMPY TOO

This is not to say, of course, that dogs are all sweetness and light. On the whole, the portrayal of canines in Western society today is positive, and dogs are usually portrayed as faithful, loving companions who are kind, noble, and can do no wrong. If a character in a story owns a dog, we can be pretty sure that we are supposed to like the character; there's just something about dogs that implies goodness.

But of course, dogs are not the embodiment of goodness; dogs do experience emotions and like humans, they are capable of getting tired and grumpy. While they are certainly able to tolerate physical conditions far worse than anything most humans would put up with, they do still get physically uncomfortable, and enough cold rain will make them just as miserable as it will us (only, of course, they don't have to clean up the muddy footprints as well).

My dogs are used to being let inside somewhere between 6pm and 7pm, after we've had time to get home from work and unwind from the day. If it hits 7pm and they're not inside yet, they'll sit as close to the door as they can and if they see us moving around, they'll whine once or twice.

If it hits 8pm and it's well and truly dark, you can guarantee the whining will be much more persistent. While this is certainly evidence of their ability to form routines amongst other things, it's also comfort-based. It's dark, it's getting cooler, and they want warmth and company. On truly miserable mornings, Laura has been known to refuse to set foot outside the door: she takes one look at the weather and something akin to 'Nuh uh, I'm not going out in that!' goes through her head.

And like humans, dogs can reach the end of their emotional tether. Although it takes a *lot* to wear out a couple of Labradors, Laura particularly is markedly more patient with prodding and poking either when she's fresh and awake (and not full of beans), or so tired it's just too much effort to tell me to go away and leave her alone.

At the end of a long day, you can *tell* when a dog is tired and grumpy, the same way you can with people. It's all in the body language; they haul themselves around like it's an effort, they give you that 'Must you?' look, and the skin under their eyes and at the upper part of their cheeks hollows and looks strained, much like humans do when they get dark circles or bags under their eyes.

- Although dogs can withstand far greater physical discomfort than your average human, they do still prefer comfort, given the choice.
- Like humans, dogs can get tired and grumpy, and this will show in their body language and behavior.

MISTAKE 4: INTELLIGENCE

This is the other Big Issue when it comes to differentiating between human and animal—especially since scientists still can't really agree on what it means to be intelligent. Society on the whole seems to recognize now that it's more than just being 'book-smart'; your EQ (emotional intelligence) is now considered just as important as your IQ. It's also fairly intuitive that people have strengths and weaknesses—individuals can have a high level of athletic talent and lack mathematical ability, or they can be good at music and terrible at writing.

This reveals one of the fundamental mistakes that we tend to make when assessing canine (and sometimes human) intelligence: we tend to assume that because dogs have comparatively low levels of, for example, linguistic intelligence, they are not intelligent at all. But in reality, like humans they have high levels of intelligence in some areas, and not in others.

They are experts in reading broad emotions and body language (one study showed that dogs are at least as accurate as humans in judging a person's character), and are highly trainable and quick to learn; they might therefore be considered to have very high levels of interpersonal intelligence.

If we base our definition of intelligence on the ability to learn, other studies suggest that dogs are one of the most intelligent non-primates, with superior intelligence to that even of large cats.

In practical terms, much of a dog's intelligence relates to a very specific and remarkable ability, which is the ability to recognize causation. They may not be able to do calculus, but they are experts at recognizing patterns of behavior.

- 'Intelligent' means different things in different circumstances.
- Dogs may not be able to parse syntax or perform calculus, but there can be no doubt that they are intelligent in other ways.

MISTAKE 5: IDENTITY AND A THEORY OF MIND

One of the greatest bones of contention (no pun intended) regarding canine intelligence relates to the concept of identity: do dogs possess self-identity? Are they self-aware? Do they, in fact, have a theory of mind, which is both the ability to attribute mental states to both oneself and others, and the assumption that other people have minds separate and distinct from our own?

It's a tricky issue. On the one hand, they lack the necessary frontal-lobe equipment to process ideas to the same extent humans can; we are far better at planning, logic and reasoning than dogs are. Dogs also fail the 'mirror test', meaning they fail to recognize themselves in mirrors, which is frequently used as a test to determine a creature's self-awareness.

We used this to our advantage at one point when the 'baby dog' Max, then a fully-grown, gripped-in-the-throes-of-adolescent-hormones eighteen-month-old, developed the disturbing habit of growling at other males; we set a mirror up next to his crate and enjoyed the entertainment when, over the next few nights, he'd accidentally catch his own eye in the mirror and start growling at the intruding dog, who of course would growl back, and the situation would escalate until he learned to calm down and control himself.

However, this lead to an interesting (and not entirely unforeseeable) result: eventually, he got used to the 'other dog' being there, and didn't bother to make eye contact or growl. But he didn't generalize this to all other dogs—just the specific male Lab that used to hang outside his crate.

This, along with various other similar experiences (such as the dislike Laura has for a particular beagle with whom Max was utterly enamored) leaves no doubt in my mind that dogs have some ability to recognize individuals.

I confess, at one point in my life I was dubious about the whole idea of puppies in particular remembering specific humans. These doubts were forever laid to rest when we had our 2011 litter of puppies. It was very early days and Laura was holed up in the litterbox. Neighbors who had never before been inside our house came to visit the newborns, and Laura—well, she wasn't terribly impressed. Barking, growling, defensive posture (an achievement for a dog lying in a box with a blanket and eight cute, furry, wriggly puppies feeding from her), the works.

I rather naively assumed that she was just being generally defensive and didn't want any visitors at all other than myself and my husband—so imagine my delight when the following day my mother arrived to visit and Laura barked and carried on until Mum came around the corner and Laura saw who it was. The change in her attitude was instant: she visibly relaxed, the barking ceased, and she wagged her tail so hard I'm glad a puppy wasn't in the way. There is no other logical explanation but that Laura recognized Mum as someone familiar and responded accordingly.

Similarly, we had the sad situation of having a pup from that litter returned to us after she had been with her new owners for three weeks. There was nothing wrong with her; they had just realized that a Labrador puppy wasn't for them. She appeared on my doorstep, a wriggling, wiggling bundle of enthusiasm, and the first thing her former-owner said was, "Wow, she certainly remembers you."

The body language of both pup and mother when they were reunited also indicated plainly that they recognized each other.

There is further evidence that dogs have some sort of theory of mind and identity: not only do they recognize individuals, both human and canine, and not only can they take a liking or disliking to specific other breeds or even other *colors* (a friend's Labrador who is wary of all white dogs, for example, after a run-in with a white dog when he was young), they also show the ability to conceive desires.

A desire is the knowledge that you want something, which obviously requires some conception of yourself as a 'you'. Dogs clearly display comfort-seeking behavior, and although this *can* be explained as a response to stimuli, there are other desire-based actions that aren't so easy to explain away. For example, Laura rings a bell that hangs on the back door to let us know that she needs to go outside (usually to relieve herself, but sometimes also for water, or simply to run around and bark at something), and when we are slow to respond, she will run back and forth between us and the door, dinging the bell ever more impatiently until finally, *finally*, we silly humans get the point; her body language makes it eminently clear that she thinks she has us trained to respond in order to fulfill her desires.

Finally, you only have to watch two dogs that are comfortable and familiar with each other interact for a length of time to see desire-based behavior at work, as well as deception, an action which is virtually impossible without some theory of mind. The young dog who tugs on the older dog's ears, cheeks, tail, whatever it can reach in an effort to lure the older dog into play; the dog who runs with their toy to the nearest playmate, human or dog, only to dodge away at the last minute; the dog who drops the toy, inviting it to be picked up, only to dive in and snatch it up at the last second and dart away; these are all examples of desire- and deception-based play that are only possible because the dog is able to conceive that the other individual involved will act separately and independently from themselves.

All of which is a very long way of saying that dogs definitely do interact with other people and other dogs as individuals, and dogs themselves can have individual personalities, quirks, and desires. (That much was obvious, right?)

- Dogs fail the mirror test, lack a developed frontal lobe and experience simple emotions; it is therefore highly unlikely that their inner lives are as rich as our own, and that they conceive of themselves as "I".
- They do, however, clearly possess some degree of a theory of mind, as they are able to recognize individuals as distinct and separate beings, and demonstrate this in their social interactions.

MISTAKE 6: GENDER

The TV program *Lassie* demonstrated quite clearly that a lot of people believe male and female dogs are interchangeable—the actual collies playing Lassie were all male (they're larger and have thicker, more impressive summer coats).

In reality, male dogs and female dogs are quite distinct. Although there are always exceptions, male dogs are usually physically larger and bulkier. It's harder to keep their attention when working obedience and simple, repetitive tasks (generally), but on the whole they are significantly better at problem-solving than females. They are often reputed to prefer being closer to their humans around the home than female dogs; however, they are less prone than females to separation anxiety and the associated behavior problems, and are more prone to aggression.

Female dogs, by contrast, are more independent. They don't need to be so close to you—as long as they know you're around somewhere, all is well. They are less likely to be reactive to situations, which contributes to their superior abilities in obedience and working tasks where focus and concentration are required, but are also less likely to care about what you think. Despite this, they are more prone to separation anxiety than male dogs. They are, however, less likely than male dogs to have behavior problems that stem from a lack of training.

Interestingly, this only holds true for the majority of dog breeds. In both poodles and English pointers, for example, males are the gentler, more trainable sex—and in many terrier breeds, there's no discernible difference between the sexes at all.

- Male and female dogs are distinctly different, though of course this is a spectrum rather than an either/or situation.
- Males are more likely to want to hang around next to you, but they are less likely to experience anxiety. Instead, they're more likely to show aggression and training-related misbehaviors, and to get distracted easily—and females are the opposite.

SECTION TWO: THE SENSES

Humans interpret more information from body language than the actual spoken words we hear; a huge percentage of communication occurs via visual means, so it's fairly intuitive that our preferred method of receiving information from the world is via our eyes.

For dogs, however, sight is secondary; the world comes alive through their sense of smell. And unlike humans, dogs have eighteen ear muscles which they can use independently; the world is a much more nuanced place when experienced through canine senses.

MISTAKE 7: SIGHT

Contrary to popular belief, dogs do not see in black and white. It's surprising, actually, that this myth has perpetuated for as long as it has; the first study to confirm that dogs could differentiate between at least some colors was done way back in 1969. Further studies have since confirmed that dogs (and probably all mammals) are what are called 'dichromats', which means (to oversimplify somewhat) that dogs have two primary colors, rather than our three.

It's basically the same thing that happens in humans with color-blindness; whereas normal-sighted humans have three different kinds of color sensors, in color-blind people one type of sensor stops working and they can only detect colors across two spectrums.

In practical terms, this means dogs can detect blue and green as separate colors, but anything in the red range appears indistinguishable from these other two. Because of this, dogs (and color-blind humans) are actually *better* at perceiving the difference between shades of grey and khaki than normal-sighted people.

But the issue of color is actually largely irrelevant to a dog. Ultimately, movement is a lot more important to dogs than color is, and in fact certain breeds of dogs, collectively called 'sight hounds' (see mistake 27), were bred especially to hunt down large prey by tracking movement. Gundogs also have this ability, tracking birds across the sky (and Laura adores the TV because it has constant movement stimulation). Dogs also have a better field of view than humans—their eyes are set further apart and slightly to the sides of their heads, though the downside of this is that their depth perception isn't as good—and although their vision isn't as crystal clear as a human with 20:20, they can see much better than we can at nighttime and in low light situations.

- Dogs do not see in black and white; rather, they see much as a color-blind human does.
- Movement is far more important than color to a dog, and they are much more sensitive to it than humans. They can also see better in low-light situations.

MISTAKE 8: SMELL

Open your eyes. Don't see.

I mean it. Keep your eyes open, and try as hard as you can not to see. If you're anything like the average human, you'll find this difficult-to-impossible to do.

That's what smell is like for a dog. It's there, all the time, something they are always conscious of, a factor that provides them with many, many times more information than their sight; whereas the human brain is dominated by a visual cortex, a dog's brain is dominated by an olfactory cortex, and it's estimated that dogs in general have a sense of smell one hundred thousand to one million times more sensitive than humans.

This is largely because canine noses are simply better built for smelling than human noses. Even the wetness of a healthy dog's nose relates to their sense of smell: a wet nose is more sensitive to air currents and, when paired with cold receptors in the skin of the nose, allow a dog to accurately pinpoint the direction a smell is coming from.

And those slits down the sides of a dog's nose? They're a nifty little design feature that allows a dog to get a noseful of scent-laden air without having to breathe in. To really understand the value of this, try to smell something *without* breathing in. For us, virtually impossible; for dogs, as easy as blinking, and something that means that scent information is passing through their brain as constantly as visual information is for us. Probably more, in fact, given we can turn off our visual information channel by closing our eyes and they can't close their noses.

It is still unknown exactly what information a dog can detect via smell, but to date they have been shown to have the ability to detect various chemicals, explosives, drugs, all sorts of foods, and even illnesses such as cancer. There is speculation that when a dog sniffs another dog's urine, they can receive information about not only the health of the other dog, their receptiveness to mating, and so forth, but also their emotional state at the time.

It has also been suggested that dogs are able to smell things as their component parts. Just as we can look at an image and see both a face and various types of fruit, dogs can smell something and recognize it as both the whole, vegetable soup, and its components: carrot, potato, garlic, and so forth.

- Dogs cannot *not* smell, just like humans cannot *not* see when their eyes are open.
- Out of all the senses, it is the nose that provides dogs with the most information—and this information might even include things like another dog's emotional state.

MISTAKE 9: SOUND

A dog's sense of hearing is its second most developed sense. Dogs are able to hear sounds between four and five times further away than the average human can, and at much higher frequencies—a range of about 40 Hz to 60,000 Hz, which is so high that humans can't hear these sounds at all.

Dogs have incredible sound discrimination abilities, and can distinguish the sound of their owner's whistle from other people's; the sound of their owner's car from other cars of the same make and model; and it's even believed by some researchers that they can detect an oncoming earthquake as much as three days ahead of time by the change in frequency of the vibrations that the earth makes.

They also have superb directional hearing. Humans have nine muscles that can move their ears, and we know how to use only one or two of those. Dogs, by contrast, have 18 (or more) muscles, and know how to use them all. As well as being able to tell what direction a sound is coming from, dogs can determine the relative size of an animal from the pitch of its voice—another reason why dogs tend to be warier of men, since their deeper voices suggest a much bigger creature than the higher voices of females.

- Dogs can hear things much further away and with a higher frequency than humans can. Because of this, they can react to things much sooner than a human can.
- Tone and pitch are important to a dog, and inform them of many subtle things, like the speaker's relative size and mood.

MISTAKE 10: TASTE

It's a common concept in our culture: the domestic dog as a garbage-guts, an eating-machine, a creature that will chomp through anything remotely food-like that's put in front of it. To a large extent it's true: watching Max eat is an experience more closely related to watching a vacuum-cleaner at work than anything remotely gustatory.

However, this is not always the case. Another dog my family owned, a Rough Collie called Mindy, was as un-food-oriented as it's possible to be without starving. A pat on the head was worth far more than a treat, and she regularly ate about half the recommended daily intake for her meals, despite maintaining a healthy weight. Laura, too, is thoroughly unusual for a Labrador in that she will self-monitor her food intake. In fact, when she was the only dog in the house-hold, we didn't bother to feed her—we simply left the open bag of dog food in a handy location inside, and she would help herself as she felt like it of an evening. Never once did we have a problem with her over-indulging!

Not only can dogs be unmotivated by food, they can also develop fussiness in terms of what they will and won't eat. In my experience, smaller dogs tend to be fussier as a very loose principle, but Laura again has demonstrated that dogs can even go through *stages* of fussiness; we spoiled her a little for a while by mixing all sorts of tasty treats in with her dry kibble, until we realised that she was developing such a liking for the tasty extras that she'd eat those and leave the kibble. She's also been known to refuse to eat when she has realised that the other dog has been fed something different that is *clearly* much tastier, and she even refused food when she realised that not only was her son Max really was staying for good, but the house we'd relocated to was also a permanent change.

These days, both the current dogs get plain, dry, high-quality kibble morning and night, with the occasional treats for training at other times, and they are both thriving. It's a common myth that dogs will get 'bored' with eating the same thing day-in, day-out, and granted, some breeds are more likely to than others, but it's also useful to remember that dogs have far less developed senses of taste than humans, and that their sense of taste, although closer to humans' than cats are, leads them to prefer different things (duck poo, anyone?). In general, a dog's opinion of what tastes good centres around sweet and savoury (umami); they don't seem to react to saltiness or sourness much at all. And while some breeds and individuals tend to be wary of any food they haven't experienced before, dogs in general are pretty terrible at learning to avoid food that makes them feel sick.

Which brings me to the final taste-related issue: although a dog *might* eat anything you place before it, it doesn't necessarily follow that what the dog is eating is *good* for it—nor does it actually follow that what it is eating is food! The top ten causes of toxicoses in dogs are: ibuprofen, chocolate, ant/roach baits, rodenticides, acetaminophen, pseudoephedrine cold medications, thyroid hormones, bleach, fertilizer, and hydrocarbons.

Two chemicals contribute to chocolate's toxicity: theobromine, the chemical that stimulates endorphin release in humans, and caffeine. Either of these chemicals independently can kill a dog in large enough doses, let alone chocolate where the two are combined. The lethal dose of milk chocolate for dogs is somewhere around 55 grams (2 ounces) per kilogram (2.2 pounds), and of course even less is needed for dark chocolate (about 6 grams per kilogram), and less still for pure cocoa powder.

Some lesser-known dog poisons include onions and garlic, some estimates suggesting that half an onion is enough to make a dog drastically ill; grapes and grape by-products, which can cause renal failure in large quantities; and cabbage. Foods that aren't necessarily poisonous but that are still bad for dogs include cooked bones, which can splinter and lodge in the dog's throat; cat food, which is too rich for dogs and can cause liver damage; and one that our family found out the hard way: corn cobs. Let's just say they make a pretty effective intestinal plug, which require surgical (read: expensive) removal.

- Not all dogs will eat all things.
- Not all things a dog eats will be good for it.

MISTAKE 11: DOGS EAT GRASS WHEN THEY'RE SICK

Yes, dogs eat grass when they're sick (one theory suggests that it's because the grass tickles the throat and stomach when gulped down, inducing vomiting, which can alleviate stomach upsets), but many dogs also graze on grass when they're feeling just fine. Why? Because dogs, unlike cats, are not carnivores; they're omnivores.

In the wild, wolves usually devour their prey whole, include stomach—and stomach contents. As most of their prey consists of herbivores, they end up getting a fair amount of second-hand roughage in their diet. Dogs, on the other hand, tend to subsist on commercial diets that, while they are usually nutritionally sound, don't quite have the same fibrous texture as raw grass. Why grass particularly? Probably because it's the most accessible plant matter. Experts suggest that if you want to avoid the dog chewing up the lawn, you can try supplementing their diet with cooked green vegies.

- Dogs can gulp down grass when they are sick to help induce vomiting.
- Dogs often graze on grass to round out their diet.

MISTAKE 12: TOUCH

Humans hug. It's what we do. It's how we show affection, camaraderie, sympathy, and a whole host of other emotions.

However, this is an all-too-familiar picture: the human grinning away, while the dog is showing whale eyes (I'm really uncomfortable, so I'll turn my head away, but I feel anxious enough to keep an eye on the situation) or just plain looking uncomfortable, and you can all but hear them thinking: "Let me go, already!"

Dogs use touch in their communication, but not in the same way we do. For us, a hug expresses affection; for a dog, it's more similar to another dog challenging them by putting its paws around their neck. Instead, dogs express affection by licking (especially the face; this is a sign of respect), flea-biting (a rapid, gentle nibble—sort of the dog equivalent of us giving them a good scratch) or snuggling (body to body, rather than with limbs, so it's non-confining and non-threatening).

The primary importance of touch for dogs is a) investigating and b) establishing boundaries, and both of these are mostly done with a dog's mouth, since they don't have hands. If they want to investigate something new, they can't feel it with fingers like we do, so they sniff at it and pick it up in their mouth. The long whiskers around their muzzle also aid in collecting information through touch.

Dogs also use their mouths to establish boundaries. Obviously, when their personal boundaries are pushed too far, they will use their teeth to make it very clear to whomever has broken the boundaries that they're not welcome. But dogs can use their mouths in more subtle ways as well. This is, in fact, one of the most important things that a puppy learns from interactions with its mother and littermates. Through play, it learns to control how hard it's biting (called bite inhibition), and learns to know the difference between a play bite, not intended to cause harm, and a real bite. A puppy that hasn't spent long enough with its littermates will often have a much more painful bite than one who has learned bite inhibition.

- Dogs lick and snuggle to show affection and submission, but they certainly don't hug.
- Because they lack hands, dogs mostly use their mouths to explore new objects.

MISTAKE 13: SHOWING PAIN

When people think of a dog in pain, they usually think of a yelp—that short, sharp, high-pitched noise somewhat reminiscent of surprise. In reality though, dogs are more often silent sufferers, which can make it very difficult to tell when a dog is in pain, or where the pain is.

Even a limp can be misleading; at one point, Laura limped every time she got up, but despite prodding and manipulation, neither we nor the vet could figure out the actual site of the pain, let alone the cause of it—and as she was moving perfectly fine again after about a week, we shook our heads and consigned it to being an unsolvable mystery. And when Laura gave birth, she yelped the very first time with the very first puppy (a very big boy who was stillborn) but otherwise was silent, apart from a very rare groan with some of the bigger pups.

Dogs show pain in a few ways. Most commonly, it's very subtle—a shift from the way they normally carry themselves, a change in behavior to being either more irritable or lethargic, eating less or perhaps being more restless, a change in their response to your petting. If the pain is more severe, they might limp or favor the area more obviously and flinch if you touch it. If it gets bad enough, they might snap at you (just as a human would, only we snap with words rather than teeth) or vocalize—from a mild whimper to a sharp yelp.

These responses lie on a spectrum, just as with humans. The difference for dogs is that vocalizing their pain is usually a last resort. A perfect example of this spectrum is the way our dogs behave when they get ear infections. Yellow Labradors are particularly prone to ear infections for some reason, and ours used to get them three or four times a year. Initially, we'd spot that they had an infection because they'd start shaking their head when they get up, or when they pause in playing. It's almost like they're trying to shake the infection out, and if you know what you're listening for you can *hear* that the ears are infected—they sound wetter and heavier than healthy ears.

The next stage is scratching, where they'll scratch at their own ears and, if you rub their ears for them, they'll grunt and lean in to the pressure. If the infection worsens from there, they'll have the opposite reaction: they'll pull away if you rub too hard near the base of their ears, and maybe give a very quiet yelp if you happen to press the wrong spot—much like a person winces and hisses if you hit a knot in the muscle when massaging.

- Dogs *do* show pain, but the threshold for showing this is much higher than for humans.
- The most frequent indicator of pain is subtle: a shift in the way they move, a slight limp, or simply favoring the area. Vocalizing their pain, especially groaning, moaning and yelping, is relatively uncommon and usually reserved for severe pain and surprise.

SECTION THREE: LEARNING AND DEVELOPMENT

As well as the way dogs experience the world, the way that they physically grow and develop throughout their lives has an impact on their personality—when it comes to nature versus nurture, I'm very firmly in the 'both' camp. The following mistakes deal with some misconceptions about canine development—everything from their relationship to wolves (more complex than people think), to that old maxim, 'You can't teach an old dog new tricks' (you absolutely can, with the right methods and the right dog).

MISTAKE 14: DOMESTICATED WOLVES

It's all very well to make the assumption that dogs are domesticated wolves (which is the accepted origin of dogs), but what people tend not to realize is the significance of such a statement. Domestication is not a one-off, reversible process; it profoundly affects the way a creature's brain operates and, correspondingly, their behavior.

In the 1940s, Russian geneticists began an experiment to domesticate silver foxes in order to breed them for their fur. By selecting for docility, they were able to develop a strain of tame silver foxes in about twenty generations. But interestingly, the tame foxes were more like dogs than their original foxy ancestors: they began to actively seek human company, wag their tails in a manner similar to dogs, lick at people's faces, and to yip and bark like dogs (and very unlike wild adult foxes and wolves, who rarely vocalize).

But the changes weren't only behavioral: some of the foxes developed floppy ears, and females began to come in season twice a year like dogs, rather than once a year like foxes. Unfortunately for the researchers, the foxes' coats also became more like those of domesticated dogs, with patches of different shades and a variety of colors.

Likewise with dogs; centuries of breeding based on humanity's desire for companionship have created a modern dog with a very different mindset to your average wolf-in-the-woods. Physically, dog skulls are about 20% smaller than wolf skulls, and dog brains are about 10% smaller than those of wolves. Their paws are about half the size, their skin is thicker, and they require fewer calories to survive than an average wolf.

Mentally, dogs are much more tractable than even tame wolves, and socially their 'pack' system is not nearly as complex or hierarchical as that of wolves. They are more responsive to coercive techniques that involve fear, aversive methods, and force, whereas wolves are more likely to just get fed up with you trying to bully them and either walk away, or bite your hand off; and dogs tend to respond to vocal cues better than wolves, who prefer hand signals. And although dogs are easier to control than wolves, a well-motivated wolf is actually easier to teach.

In a way, you might think of wolves as fully-developed adults, and dogs as over-grown puppies. In fact, breeding for domesticity is in many ways breeding for permanent puppyhood; dogs are smaller than their wild counterparts (generally), have markedly shorter (more puppy-like) muzzles, have lop ears in some breeds, lick people's faces (which puppies do to their parents both to show respect and to encourage their parent to regurgitate food for them), have the puppyish characteristics of submissiveness, tractability and dependency, love to play, and have a comparatively high tolerance for new situations, things and people.

This does not make dogs somehow less than wolves, and neither does it make wolves superior, any more than children or adults are superior to one another. They are different, unique, and fulfill different roles in the world.

- Dogs are presumed to have evolved from wolves, but they are not wolves; domestication changes a creature both physically and behaviorally—permanently.
- In many ways, in terms of their social, emotional and cognitive skills, the relationship between dog and wolf is akin to that of child and adult.

MISTAKE 15: AGE, GROWTH AND MATURITY

Lots of people seem to equate growth with maturity. Once the dog is fully grown—usually between twelve and twenty months—people tend to assume that they are now an adult, and expect them to act accordingly. But this is not the case.

Look at human children: they may hit puberty anywhere between the ages of ten and sixteen, but we don't consider them an adult until their early 20's. And even then, we're placing some weighty expectations on them: while our physical bodies are well and truly done growing by age twenty, our brains continue to develop. The frontal lobe (the rationalizing, planning, and fore-thinking part) isn't fully developed in females until about age 23, and males until about age 25.

Like humans, dogs remain 'children' long after their bodies stop growing. And just as people reach mental maturity at different rates, so do dogs. Some of this is based on the breed—Labradors, for example, are notorious for retaining puppy-like enthusiasm and behavior until at least the age of three—and some of it is based on the individual's personality, and also on external factors. Laura the Labrador calmed down much quicker than her sister Abbi did, and ceased the annoying puppy behaviors like unwanted chewing and digging sooner. However, she retained a puppy-like enthusiasm for games and attention, and despite our best efforts still jumps like she has springs in her feet—which just goes to show that dog personalities can be every bit as complex as human personalities. And once Laura had a permanent playmate who *was* a puppy, some of her (annoying) puppy tendencies—digging, tearing washing off the line—returned or increased, such that Abbi, a solo dog, is now much calmer and more mature in all aspects.

- Dogs continue to mature mentally after they have matured physically.
- Different dogs will 'grow up' at different speeds, and some may never outgrow their 'puppy' habits.

MISTAKE 16: IMPRINTING AND INSTINCT

Instinct. We all know dogs have it, but what does that *mean*, exactly? How does it feel to have a dog's instincts? How does it affect them as individuals, and how does it shape their personalities? And what on earth is imprinting?

Imprinting has to do with the very first lessons any creature learns once it's born: the things that are imprinted on its mind before it even knows it has one, before it realizes that it can interact with its environment. It's how a puppy learns to recognize its mother, how it learns where to find food, and how it's comforted by its littermates as they huddle together in a squiggling mass of puppy pile. It's how a dog might learn to be afraid of loud noises (although unless this fear is reinforced as it grows, it's likely to forget this), and how it can develop either into a dog that deals well with stress and separation—a puppy who's experienced mild stress as a neonate will cope with it much better as an adult—or one who melts at the first sign of tension.

Instinct, on the other hand, is the things a creature knows without needing to learn. The drive of a hunter to chase things, the instinct of an animal trying to conserve its food to dig and bury. It's the confidence of a predator that it's designed to fight if it wants to, and the sense of pack that animals who hunt together have—although the pack instinct is weaker in dogs than in wolves due to the effects of domestication. A beautiful example of the latter was the way in which our one-year-old entire male Max interacted with his younger siblings when they came along. Despite his usual goofy propensities and general lack of spatial awareness, Max treated the tiny baby puppies with the utmost care, treading carefully and deliberately (highly unusual for him!) and letting them ramble all over him, even chewing on his tail, without moving a muscle—the behavior of a creature that clearly knows the importance and fragility of the young.

We all know what the basic instincts of a dog are; as a writer, make sure you let these instincts impact the way your dog characters see and interact with the world.

- Imprinting is the learning a dog does before it's old enough to realize it can interact with its environment.
- Instinct is the things a dog knows without having to learn. Both of these things dramatically shape the way a dog views the world.

MISTAKE 17: CANINE VERSUS FELINE

Although the rivalry between cat and dog is entrenched in our culture (even manifesting in people—we can be either dog or cat people; society rarely accepts a profession to be both), those of you that are privileged to have owned both a dog and a cat at the same time will know that there are two sides to every story.

Yes, dogs chase cats. But it is my belief that the reason for this is *not* primarily because they are cats: it is primarily because they *run*. When Laura was a very small puppy, we took her to visit my in-laws. They owned a rather large tabby cat, who is rather used to getting his own way—and this young upstart of a pup, with her over-exuberant and playful nature, was nothing but an irritation to the older cat. So, one day, when Laura got just that little bit too close, the cat took a swipe— and Laura learned the hard way that you don't approach cats unwarily.

The collie we had as a family when my baby sister was young used to babysit the family guinea pigs, lying perfectly still as they crawled all over her, squeaking and squealing and snuffling. A beagle that we owned when I was small became best friends with our large grey rabbit. They used to lie quite happily side-by-side in the sun, completely at peace with each other, despite their predator-and-prey relationship. And Abbi, my mother's Labrador Retriever, is quite content to ignore the fluffy brown-and-white rabbit that shares her yard (in a hutch!).

What do all these scenarios have in common? In all instances, the non-dog didn't run. They didn't act like prey—so the dog didn't treat them like prey. Abbi is a perfect example: she will ignore the rabbit… until it runs.

Dogs and cats are perfectly able to get along with each other—provided that one or the other has learned either to not run, or to not chase things that run.

- Dogs generally don't chase cats because they're cats; they chase them because they run.
- If prey animals don't act like prey, dogs generally won't treat them like prey.

MISTAKE 18: CAUSATION

Causation is the way in which something causes something else to happen: if I touch something hot, it will hurt. The heat causes me pain. The act of touching *causes* me pain.

As humans, we're both very unobservant about causation, and very good at inventing it. Our bodies just aren't equipped to acutely monitor things like air pressure, ensuing tidal waves, or the cause of black holes, so we often miss environmental clues that other animals find obvious. We're pretty good at *inventing* causation though, when we feel we need it: If only I hadn't decided to go down to the shops, I wouldn't have had that car accident, and Billy would still be alive (I *caused* Billy's death)... If only I hadn't met John at the supermarket, I wouldn't have felt depressed and eaten the entire tub of chocolate ice cream (John *caused* my weight gain)...

Dogs, on the other hand, are well-equipped to notice even minute changes in everything from the weather to someone's body language. A lot of their 'intelligence' is actually a remarkable ability to notice things and to associate them through causation.

For instance, have you ever noticed how excited a dog gets when you pick up its leash and head towards your shoes, as opposed to the merely hopeful look it gives you if you're heading in the wrong direction? Humans are creatures of habit, and even though most of the time *we're* not aware of our habits, dogs are.

An excellent example of the associative abilities of animals is Clever Hans, a horse who was famous for being able to add and subtract, indicating his answer by tapping his hoof the correct number of times—until observers realized that he was actually picking up an unconscious cue that his trainer offered whenever he'd reached the correct number of taps.

An example of the power of associative learning is Martin Seligman's experiments that formed the foundation of the theory of learned helplessness. A dog was conditioned to associate a particular sound with an electric shock, and was prevented from evading it. Once the association had been formed, the scenario was changed: if the dog jumped over a low divider within ten seconds of hearing the sound, it would be able to avoid the shock—but because it had previously learned that nothing it did mattered, it didn't even attempt to escape.

Because dogs' ability to learn associatively is so strong, it can cause a multitude of problems during training; not only do dogs quickly develop these associations, they are also extremely sensitive to both substrate (the surface they're standing on) and orientation (the direction they're facing). Sit on the grass isn't sit on the concrete. Lie on the mat isn't lie on the stairs. Stand facing north isn't stand facing south, jump off the chair isn't jump off the table, go through a doorway isn't go through a tunnel, and so on, and so on, and so on.

Some dogs will generalize pretty quickly—others will drive you batty with their specificity. And of course, they don't generalize all commands equally: Laura learned very quickly that 'leave it' meant leave *whatever* I was indicating, but trying to teach her that 'stay' meant 'hold *whatever* position you are in', not 'stay sitting', took forever. If you want to go moderately insane, try to teach a dog to follow the direction of your pointing finger!

A quick side note about training: there are lots of training methods that have been used with dogs throughout history, and it's rare for two people to ever agree completely about the best way to approach the task of teaching something to a dog. The most important thing to remember is to keep the training method appropriate to your context—both the type of character in question, and the history and societal context in which they exist. And regardless of the method used, dogs are usually quite willing to do what a human asks of them, provided that they first of all understand what is being asked, and second of all have not been provided with too many reasons throughout their life to ignore such requests (abuse, lack of pay-off, etc.).

- Dogs learn through association, but the chain of causation that they end up with isn't necessarily going to be based on true cause-and-effect—it's outcomes-based, but the dog's definition of a good outcome and your definition (or your character's) may differ significantly.
- Dogs are extremely aware of both substrate and orientation, and have to be taught to generalize commands on a range of surfaces, and facing a range of directions.

MISTAKE 19: MEMORY AND REWARDS

Dogs aren't famed for their memory as elephants, but the everyday successes that people have in training dogs proves, I think, their remarkable memory. Laura learned to go out and around a pole on command in just three half-hour sessions, spread out over two months. And I'm sure we've all heard the amazing stories of dogs who get lost, only to find their way home again from incredible distances. If ever I thought that dogs didn't know where home was, the Labrador once again convinced me: she knows from the smell where we are driving, and has a different kind of response accordingly—whether it's the dog park, her sister's house, a long trip to the coast, or home.

Dogs learn. Dogs remember. Their ability to pick things up quickly and remember them is closely linked to causation. They remember what worked—and what didn't. Humans do this too, just much more subconsciously. If a dog does something and gets a good result, it is much more likely to repeat the action. If, by contrast, it doesn't get a good result, then it will be less likely to repeat that action.

Remember that the dog is the one that defines a successful and unsuccessful action: while we may think jumping up on a stranger is a very *un*successful thing to do, if the dog gets patted by said stranger or in some other way gets attention, then, ta da! Mission accomplished: it wanted attention, and it got it. This is a classic example of how bad habits can form through accidental reinforcement.

- Although it's not often mentioned, dogs have excellent memories.
- Dogs are particularly attuned to remembering which actions of theirs brought about successful results, and which didn't—and they're more likely to repeat an action that gets them results.

MISTAKE 20: DOMINANCE AND SUBMISSION

Dogs are very hierarchical as a general rule, but it's vitally important to remember that in the dog world, 'to be in charge of' is synonymous with 'to take care of'. If the leader, be they human or canine, is too harsh and doesn't actually act in the best interest of the pack, a rebellion can occur. Dogs will challenge another dog by testing their boundaries, and they'll do the same with a person: climbing onto furniture and/or attempting to claim the bed (both attempts to claim the most comfortable seating); nipping or 'holding' hands; making first claim on food, toys or other resources; and so on. In extreme cases, owners have even reported being harassed by their dogs, who will bark, growl and snap to get their human to 'behave'.

Interestingly, the same thing can happen if the leader is too soft. Being too doting towards a dog mimics the behavior of a submissive pack member; from their perspective, rather than demonstrating to them that you care, you are asking to be taken care of. The idea of being the boss of your household pack may terrify your dog stupid, but they will do it regardless, because better a terrified leader than none at all. This situation can actually lead to worse behavior problems (even to the point of growling and snapping, as above) than the former issue, and in my opinion, based on wide reading and personal experience, is by far the more common of the two.

However, the fact that the dog recognizes that you are the leader of its pack doesn't preclude other dominance/submission issues, because dominance is a complicated thing, and it involves the hierarchy of everyone, not just the leader. Our Labradors used to vie for leadership until Laura made it clear that even though she would tolerate Max taking the lead in some areas, she was the boss overall. Unfortunately, this seemed to mean to Laura that she had to go out of her way to be dominant towards all other dogs, and managed to get her eyelid torn in a tussle with her sister. So you can see, 'dominance' is actually a complicated thing, and the dog who is boss in the lounge room might not be boss in the backyard.

- A person who is overly dominant towards their dogs will tend to inspire either fear or an eventual challenge. However, being overly submissive isn't the answer either, as the dog will then tend to assume that you need to be taken care of.
- Dominance is a complicated concept, not a once the boss, always the boss idea.

MISTAKE 21: YOU CAN'T TEACH AN OLD DOG NEW TRICKS

Dogs, like humans, have different learning styles. Ultimately, it's all based on causation, but what works with one dog may not work with another. What one dog generalizes, another may keep specific until you teach it otherwise.

But what dogs do have in common is this: almost every dog can be taught to do anything you can think of, assuming of course that it's physically possible. And unless they have been taught otherwise through negative experiences, most dogs are eager to please—sometimes *too* eager. There's nothing more hilarious than a dog who is so eager to learn that they become hyperactive and flip out, trying every behavior they can think of to see if it's what you want, without pausing to take note of what it is that you're actually saying (oh yes, I've definitely owned that dog).

Mostly, dogs will perform if they think there's something in it for them—but what is a reward for one dog may be a punishment for another (think of rewarding an extrovert by letting them have time alone in their room, or of rewarding an introvert by letting them go to a party).

So you absolutely *can* teach an old dog new tricks, but it

can be a slow and gradual process as the dog unlearns old habits—and of course, the dog might decide that the rewards aren't worth it, and it doesn't want to learn. You can teach an old dog, but you can't teach anyone, human or otherwise, who doesn't want to learn.

- Old dogs are absolutely capable of learning new tricks, and most dogs retain their eagerness to learn throughout their lives.
- Teaching any dog is a matter of finding a reward great enough to balance the hard work of learning.

SECTION FOUR: COMMUNICATION

Communication is where a lot of mistakes concerning dogs occur; in fact, it's my personal belief that if everyone was taught to really speak Dog, incidents of dog attacks and bites and the like would almost disappear.

Most of the problems here occur when people assume that because dogs are very like us, they are entirely like us, and therefore communicate in the same way. As the following mistakes will explore, there are many similarities between canine and human communication—but there are also distinct differences.

MISTAKE 22: MY DOG SPEAKS ENGLISH—LINGUISTIC INTELLIGENCE

Repeat after me: dogs do not speak English. Or Spanish, or French, or Swahili. Dogs do not speak. They most definitely communicate, but they do not speak; they have no capacity for the complex phenomenon humans call language. This is perhaps one of the biggest mistakes that people make with their dogs.

"Oh," they say, "I *know* dogs don't speak English... But my Fluffy, he's different. He's special. He just tilts his little head when I talk to him and I just *know* he *understands*."

And maybe, just maybe, he does... But what he is understanding has very little to do with the words issuing out of a human mouth, and a whole lot more to do with all the non-verbal communication that's accompanying the words: the intonation, the body language, the context.

There is no doubt at all that a dog can be *trained* to understand human language. But even that is a misleading statement: the dog is not understanding the language so much as making word associations. "Ah, when my owner makes *that* funny sound, it means he wants me to lie down. I get it, now!" It's causation again.

COMMUNICATION

Depending on your definition, this may or may not be classified as linguistic intelligence—and arguments abound for both sides of the debate. But even if you do class this as linguistic ability—whee, my dog speaks English after all!—it's a limited ability. Dogs can most certainly understand particular words or phrases that they have been trained to associate with an event; what they cannot do is parse the sentence that contains the command, breaking it down into component parts and rearranging it for meaning. When I tell my dog, "Go to mat!", she does not hear a complete imperative phrase, consisting of a verb, a preposition, and a noun; she hears a single series of sounds that indicate that if she finds her bed and lies in it, she will be rewarded.

Although we have been conditioned to believe otherwise through countless episodes of programs like *Lassie, Rin Tin Tin* and *Inspector Rex*, giving your dog a complex paragraph of instructions is more likely to leave your dog staring up at you, goofy grin on her face as she wags her tail slowly, saying, "You know what, I *think* you want me to do something…" than is it to motivate your dog to rush off and commit some daring act of heroism.

- Dogs cannot understand language in terms of breaking it down into component parts and manipulating those parts.
- Dogs can be trained to associate particular words with particular actions or 'meanings'.

MISTAKE 23: DOG TO DOG

One of the first things dogs will do when they meet is give each other a good once-over with the canine equivalent of a handshake: The Sniff. By now you'll understand that they are gleaning an enormous amount of information just from this quick once over—everything from the new dog's age and sex to the type of food they eat, and potentially their health and emotional state.

But a polite dog doesn't just rush up to another dog and start sniffing. Sure, dogs *do* this—but some humans also walk up to you and get right into your personal space they first time they meet you, too. Doesn't mean we like it.

Polite communication in the dog world consists of subtleties, not loud, outrageous gestures. When polite dogs meet, they sidle up to each other, never approaching head on, and only making the most fleeting eye contact. The younger dog, if it's been well socialized, will usually duck its head and try to lick the underside of the older dog's muzzle if it's allowed close enough—code for 'I respect you, recognize that you have authority over me, and am willing to let you be in charge'. Check out a litter of puppies adoring their older sibling some time, if you can!

As when dogs are communicating with humans, rolling onto their back around another dog can either be an invitation to play or a sign of fear or submission. Direct eye contact usually indicates a challenge (note that this isn't always the case with humans; a lot of competition obedience dogs are taught to make eye contact as a method of focusing the dog on their handler during training.

Laura especially will stare at me for minutes at a time if she thinks it'll get her a treat), licking is a sign of affection, and soft growling accompanied by ear-tugging—or any other sort of tugging or jumping, really—is asking for play. It's pretty logical: a relaxed, loose body is a relaxed, happy dog. A tense body is a tense dog, either because they're afraid, angry, or alert.

Oh, and humping? It's not all about sex at all. Unless we're talking about a male dog and an in-season female, it's actually usually a way to show dominance over the over dog, which is why female dogs do it too. The scratching the ground thing that some dogs do after they pee? That's dominance, too. All dogs have scent glands in their feet (which, incidentally, make their feet smell like corn chips, honest-to-goodness), and scratching like that is a way of making sure that their scent is unmistakable, declaring to the world, 'Here I am! Come and take me if you're hard enough!'

- Polite canine communication is all about subtlety.
- Relaxed body equals relaxed dog; tense body equals tense dog.

MISTAKE 24: DOG TO HUMAN

As humans, we tend to assume that 'communication' equals 'verbal communication'. This, however, is not true. Scientists estimate that as much as 70% of all our communication comes from what accompanies the words we hear—the tone and pitch of the speech, and body language.

In a similar way, dogs do use vocal signals to convey information, but the majority of their communication is based on body language. The difference is, dogs are hyper-aware of body language and its meaning, whereas we humans are often oblivious. Ears, eyebrows, forehead, tail—almost every part of the dog's body is used deliberately to communicate. And although it takes a bit of getting used to, it's actually pretty easy to understand what a dog is saying; there's no mistaking the happy, confident smile of a relaxed dog, or the slinking, submissive stance of a fearful dog, or the alert expression of a dog focusing on something.

There are a couple of things, though, that many people aren't aware of which are very good indicators of a dog's mood. We all know what a growl or snarl looks like, with bared teeth and raised lips—but did you know that you can tell whether a dog is growling out of terror or aggression just by looking at the corners of its mouth? If the corners are pulled forward, then the dog is angry, assertive, and ready for aggression. If, however, the corners are pulled way back, the dog is terrified, and is growling out of sheer desperation for whatever it's scared of to go away. It might also resort to aggression, but from completely different motivation.

Another good indicator is the freeze. Because dogs are much more aware of body language than humans are, they pick up on things a lot faster, so their body language doesn't have to be pronounced—but if you carefully watch a group of dogs for long enough, you're pretty much guaranteed to see one of them freeze, just for an instant, and probably glaring at another dog at the same time. That's a classic warning for the other dog to stop what it's doing and leave it alone. This is an important thing to be able to spot, because it's also a good indicator that a dog is in an uncomfortable situation and may attack; if people were better at spotting the freeze, they'd be able to tell instantly that the dog they were approaching was uncomfortable, and the vast majority of dog bites would be prevented.

Although I can't possibly do justice to canine communication in one short mistake, here are a couple of useful tidbits to end on: a dog licking its own nose is often a sign of submission, or at the very least pacification—trying to calm the situation down.

Yawning can often mean the same thing, rather than indicating tiredness. Sneezing can be a response to stress and anxiety, rolling onto the back and exposing the stomach is either an invitation to scratch *or* a pretty loud request for you to back off—and you'd better know which it is before bending over to pat (check the mouth—is the dog smiling or not?)—and a tail frozen up in the air is more likely to mean that the dog is concentrating than that the dog is happy (and if the dog is also standing with their weight and ears forward, they are on alert).

And growling can mean a whole variety of things, depending on tone and context. It's a normal part of play, and play-growling tends to be more sporadic and rumbly than fearful or aggressive growling, which often starts slowly and progressively builds. Annoyed growling is intense but brief, and to a dog, that low, rumbly thunder sounds exactly like protective growling—periodic, low-pitched—which means they can sit there quite happily growling back at the storm.

- The majority of dog-to-dog communication is non-verbal—just like humans. The difference is that dogs are hyper-aware of this.
- Language is contextual; the same action (or sound) in one context might mean something different in another context.

MISTAKE 25: HUMAN TO DOG

Despite the fact that canine and human body language is fundamentally the same—relaxed body, relaxed creature; tense body, tense creature—there are still significant differences in the way we act.

Humans, for example, don't generally tend to pee on things as a way of asserting their dominance, or sniff toilet spots to get the local goss (although writing on toilet walls might be the equivalent…?), and since we rely primarily on visual and verbal communication, we don't tend to sniff each other either. Unfortunately, this leads to more than a few misunderstandings when human and canine meet.

People hugging their dog tightly against them; people striding directly up to a dog while making eye contact; people who reach down and pat the dog firmly on top of their head; people who loom over a dog and coo, simultaneously sending the signals that they are both large and threatening, and submissive…

Any of the above scenarios could turn out to be nothing, but in the right context with the right dog, they could end in an attack—or anything in between.

So, if the words we say are largely meaningless and so much of our body language is completely off, what are our dogs responding to?

Tone of voice, for one thing. One of my friend's dogs has learned the word 'kitchen', meaning, "Stop whatever you are doing right this instance and get thee to the kitchen!" However, throwing out a neutral, off-hand 'kitchen' will elicit a completely different response to a long, drawn-out, horrified, how-could-you-possibly-do-this-to-me, 'kiiiiiiitchen!' In both cases, the instruction is the same, but the difference in tone and intonation signals to the dog a lot about how the person is feeling at the time.

And it turns dogs are pretty good at reading human emotion—much better than we are at reading theirs. In fact, some studies have shown that dogs can read the emotion on a human's face as successfully as another human can, making the way you're feeling at the time possibly the most important aspect of your communication.

- As with humans, body language is vitally important in how we communicate with dogs—we just often get it wrong.
- What we can't miscommunicate, however, is how we're feeling; given dogs' superior sense of smell and the fact that they are more highly attuned to body language, they're probably better than we are at picking up on how people are feeling.

COMMUNICATION

MISTAKE 26: TALKING ABOUT DOGS

To round out the section on communication, here's a quick gloss of words used when communicating *about* dogs.

At stud: (adjective) dogs are not studs, they are *at stud*. Same with horses, cattle, etc.

Bitch: (noun) female canine.

Conformation: (noun and adjective) the way in which a dog is put together structurally; that dog has excellent conformation, that dog does well in the conformation ring.

Dam: (noun) mother dog.

Dog: (noun) all canines, or more specifically, male canines.

Entire: (adjective) not neutered.

Gait: (noun and adjective) manner of movement; specifically the trotting pace used in showing.

Recall: (noun) the formal act of 'coming' as in competition obedience; that dog did a perfect recall.

Sire: (noun) father dog.

Stack: (noun and verb) standing in a way so as to best show off conformation; put your dog in a show stack, to stack your dog, that dog stacks well, etc.

Whelp: (verb) have puppies, give birth.

SECTION FIVE: PEDIGREES AND BREEDING

Despite the fact that all dogs are the same species, *Canis familiaris*, they show an enormous variation in appearance. In fact, dogs are the only animal to show such a huge variety of forms without speciating. However, even though all breeds are the same species, they are in many ways very different creatures, with different sets of instincts, personalities, and consequently roles in society.

Contrary to popular opinion, breeding is both an art and a science; it's not just something anyone with a female dog in season can (should) do. A lot of the knowledge required to breed responsibly is both technical, and irrelevant to writing, so I won't discuss it here. If you're interested in the topic, pick up a copy of *Canine Reproduction and Whelping: A Dog Breeder's Guide*, by Myra Savant-Harris—or any one of numerous, well-written books on this subject.

In this section, we'll have a look at misconceptions people have around neutering, general conceptions about pregnancy, labor and puppies, and we'll end by taking a look at the whole concept of a 'mongrel'.

MISTAKE 27: THE BREEDS

Dogs are not interchangeable, any more than humans are; an Irish Wolfhound is very different to a Chihuahua., not just in terms of shape and size, but also personality.

On a fundamental level, it never hurts to remember that we have so many different breeds mostly because they were bred for different jobs. This shows through in their respective personalities: hounds hunt, terriers dig, retrievers retrieve, pointers point, herders herd. The dog's breed can play a large role in determining their personality, just as a person's nationality and cultural heritage can impact their personality.

However, like nationality, breed is not a distinct, defined box. Terriers are more likely to dig than other dogs, but that doesn't mean that other dogs won't dig, or that you won't find a terrier that doesn't like digging. A prime example of this is my Labrador Laura and her sister Abbi. Labs are bred as gundogs, designed to help their master by flushing out prey (usually birds) and then retrieving it from where it falls, often from water. It is thus a requirement of any working Lab that they be a good swimmer. So generally, Labs will like water. Laura is a complete water-baby; if there's a puddle nearby, you can't keep her away from it. Seriously. I've seen her try to swim in a puddle a couple of hand-spans across. Abbi, on the other hand, can take or leave it. She's not scared of swimming, and she's competent, but she doesn't leap into it with the full-bodied waggling joy that Laura does. And Max? He just waits in ambush in the shallows for someone else to bring in the stick.

Nonetheless, there are certain observable trends across groups of breeds. There are different ways of categorizing dog breeds and many countries have their own system (Wikipedia does a good job of comparing and contrasting them). However, international bodies recognize ten different groups, each bred for different purposes:

- Sheepdogs and cattle dogs (bred for herding sheep and cattle; strong herding instinct; generally tolerant of other animals though breeds vary regarding whether they will coexist peacefully or be aroused and attempt to herd; highly trainable; energetic);
- Pinschers, Schnauzers, Molossoid Breeds, Swiss Mountain and Swiss Cattle Dogs (bred for protection; generally more aloof—tend to attach to 'their' people and not take so easily to strangers; protective of their people and space; usually large; usually build for endurance rather than speed or energy);
- Terriers (bred to hunt rabbits and the like; usually small to fit down burrows; often have wiry hair that fringes over eyes to protect from dirt; strong digging instinct; strong predator instinct, especially for small moving things—highly aroused by the presence of other animals; high energy);
- Dachshunds (bred to hunt prey, especially badgers, by scent, then follow it into its burrows;

like scenthounds, easily distracted by smells; like terriers, have a strong digging instinct; strong predator instinct; shape designed to help them fit down burrows);
- Spitz and Primitive Types (bred predominantly for sledding and hunting; spitzes are characterized by thick, double coats; usually medium build, balancing strength with efficiency; are the least likely of all groups to bark—this group contains dogs known to never bark; contains breeds most likely to howl; tend to work well with humans although may not be stranger or child tolerant, depending on individual);
- Scenthounds (bred to hunt by scent; easily distracted from humans by interesting smells; tend to be more independent and less overtly affectionate towards humans, as scenthound breeds were often bred to be kept in dog packs in kennels; most highly developed sense of smell of all dogs; built for endurance in order to be able to follow a scent trail over a long distance; some breeds have long floppy ears that aid in sweeping scents towards the nose);
- Pointing Dogs (bred to assist hunters by adopting a 'pointing' stance when they sense prey; can detect prey by smell and sight; sensitive to and aroused by the presence of other animals; usually friendly and well-disposed to all people; medium build, often tending towards long-legged in order to cover terrain);
- Retrievers, Flushing Dogs and Water Dogs (Retrievers and Flushers bred to assist hunters by flushing out game or retrieving it; Water Dogs

bred to retriever from water, either game or, for example, fishing nets, in order to assist fisherman in bringing heavy nets back to the boat; strong 'fetch' instinct; highly aroused by other animals; like Pointing Dogs, usually friendly and well-disposed to all people; highly trainable and very quick learners—some of the best obedience dogs are found in this group; energetic, though generally not as high-energy as Terriers or Herding Dogs);

- Companion and Toy Dogs (bred for companionship; generally small—'lap dogs'; vary dramatically in trainability; vary also in friendliness—some are highly people-oriented, some are more aloof and attach only to their owner; some are miniaturized versions of larger breeds; this is the group that is the least cohesive in terms of personality); and
- Sighthounds (bred to hunt by sight; extremely fast and agile; lightweight build to accommodate speed; movement-oriented and aroused by movement; strong chase instinct for things that move; tend to be some of the more aloof breeds, along with dogs from Group 2).

- Dog breeds are not interchangeable in their personality any more than in their appearance.
- Regardless, dogs are all individuals.

MISTAKE 28: MONGRELS

Mongrels: they're everywhere. But not all mongrels are equal. First of all, not all mongrels are mangy, ragged hairballs, and not all mongrels grow to a monstrous size! Mixed-breed dogs are exactly that—a mixture of breeds—and what they look like will depend on which breeds they are a mix of. Thus, mixed-breeds can be tiny, large, or just plain average. They can have short hair, long hair, wiry hair or soft hair. They can have long tails, short tails, long ears, floppy ears, pointed ears, tiny ears, snub noses, long muzzles, deep chests, skinny chests... They can have anything at all, depending on what breeds are in their genetic make-up.

Secondly, as discussed earlier, purebred dogs were bred into specific breeds for specific reasons. Every breed you can think of was someone's idea of the perfect dog for a particular task, and because of this they have the physique that most suits that task. Huskies and malamutes, who pull sleds over snow and ice, have thick, double-insulated coats that keep them warm, muscular frames that are a balance between strength and energy conservation, and extra hair between the pads on their feet to protect against ice. Greyhounds, bred to chase rabbits and thus required to run extremely fast, are lithe, agile, and light weight. Terriers, bred to chase small animals down their burrows, are small (to fit down the burrow) and hairy (to protect skin and face from dirt), and love to dig.

Mongrels, by contrast, are not bred with a specific task in mind. Couple this with the fact that there is no law that says only good qualities must be inherited, and you are bound and determined to end up with dogs who are ill-suited to anything. Of course, you'll get the opposite, too—dogs which are stunning and physically impressive, and who can adapt to just about anything—but they won't have been bred with a specific task in mind. There are pros and cons to both sides of this: the more specialized the task that a dog is bred for is, the less flexible and able to perform *other* tasks the dog will be. On the other hand, any dog with overall good conformation will be able to perform a variety of tasks.

- A conformationally sound, well-built dog will be able to perform a variety of tasks—and the more specialized the bred, the less flexible it will be.
- Mongrels don't exclusively inherit the best qualities of their parents; they are frequently oddly proportioned and vary dramatically in appearance.

MISTAKE 29: BAD HABITS

A dog isn't usually born with his bad habits intact. Sure, some dogs might have a predisposition to certain kinds of behavior that we find irritating—hound dogs who chase the rabbit around its cage, for example, or herding dogs who, even though they are obedience angels incarnate in every other aspect, refuse to walk right by our side (yes, I've owned both those dogs). But on the whole, bad habits are developed and reinforced as a dog grows.

I mentioned earlier the role that imprinting has on a dog's personality; naturally, it also has an impact on its behavior. As puppies grow, they go through what are known as 'fear periods'. During these periods, they are more susceptible to experiencing fear. They are less bold, clingier, and are generally more timid than usual. If a puppy has a negative experience during one of these periods, it can be enough to create a life-long phobia, which may induce bad habits.

Although I mentioned earlier that dogs tend not to generalize as much as humans do, it's one of the quirks of life that they are much better at generalizing fear than anything else. A car backfired and scared me while I was walking? Great. Now I'm afraid of door banging, thunder, shouting—oh yeah, and cars.

Place that dog on a narrow sidewalk with a wall on one side, a noisy truck racing past on the other, and a large man coming towards it. The man speaks with a loud, booming voice, and reaches towards the dog, who, feeling trapped, lunges out at the man's hand. Dog is punished by owner; dog is now terrified of large men. You can see how, in a particularly nervous dog, the cycle can grow and develop.

Of course, bad habits have their roots in 'nature' as much as 'nurture'. I mentioned above some of the bad habits that might develop in some breeds due to the jobs that they were originally bred for (because no behavior is bad in and of itself; it's only when we don't *want* the dog doing what it was originally bred for that it becomes a bad habit!), and there are a host of other 'bad habits' that dogs have simply because they are dogs. Licking their bottoms, for example; how else is a dog to get clean, really? The poo obsession; given the host of information they receive via it, I can understand why they want to sniff it. (Still not sure why they have to eat it, though!) Rolling in stinky substances (including poo); this is assumed to be a left-over behavior from wolf days, when disguising one's scent made hunting easier and protecting the location of the pack (and puppies) easier.

- Some habits that humans class as 'bad' are simply a result of the dog's breeding (herders herd, hounds hunt, guard-dogs guard) or the simple fact that they are dogs.
- Other habits form as a result of the dog's experiences: some bad habits are accidentally reinforced, and others form because of traumatic events.

MISTAKE 30: NEUTERING

"I can't neuter my dog! It's not fair to him!"
"I should let my dog have one litter of puppies before I neuter her."
"How would *you* like it if someone cut off your private parts?"

Excuses like these abound whenever that terrifying word, 'neuter', rears its head—particularly when the dog and human in question are both male. There's just something about the male ego that often finds the idea of neutering a male dog offensive, and even morally wrong. Sadly, this misconception is contributing factor in the huge number of puppies born, abandoned, and put down every year.

However, supporters who argue adamantly that all dogs must be neutered, (registered breeding animals aside) regardless of circumstance, and wave pictures in people's faces of baskets of cute puppies, shouting loudly about unwanted litters and euthanasia statistics, are equally guilty of resorting to emotional appeals rather than logic in support of their cause. Yes, many, many dogs are put down every year because no one wants them, and I think it's fairly obvious that even 'just one litter' can contribute signify-cantly to this number (especially if the puppies from that litter go on to have 'just one litter'). But what about the claims that neutering/spaying is actually better for the dog? Here's the real deal on neutering and spaying:

PROS

- The entire procedure is performed under general anesthetic and has a quick recovery time—it's not like the horror stories you've heard of men who've had vasectomies and walked around in agony for weeks after.
- Neutering a dog protects against testicular cancer, prostate disease, and hernias. It can also reduce anxiety, aggression, and inappropriate marking (i.e., peeing on everything they see, their humans included).
- Spaying a female, especially before her first season, helps prevent uterine infections and mammary cancer.
- Having a litter before spaying does nothing for the dog except subject it to the stress and health risks associated with pregnancy and litter-raising.
- In the majority of breeds, a neutered dog will not gain weight any differently than an entire dog.

CONS

- Neutering/spaying before one year of age significantly increases the risk of bone cancer.
- Neutering/spaying increases the risk of hypothyroidism by about three times.
- In male dogs, neutering increases the risk of progressive cognitive impairment due to age, and significantly increases the risk of obesity. It

also increases the very small risk of prostate cancer and urinary tract cancer.
- In female dogs, spaying increases the risk of cardiac hemangiosarcoma (a relatively common cancer) by possibly more than five times, increases urinary 'spay incontinence' in between 4 and 20% of bitches, and increases the risk of urinary tract infections and vaginal dermatitis.

On balance, an examination of the risks suggests that female dogs will live a healthier life if they are spayed; for males, though, the risks probably outweigh the benefits. So in order to prevent hosts of unwanted litters and decrease the euthanasia rate, it seems we need to focus on spaying the girls.

Of course, if you discount obesity (and the illnesses caused primarily by weight), the health risks associated with neutering in males are probably not as troublesome as keeping an entire dog in your yard who wants to get at every in-season female (though we spayed all the females, so this might not be such an issue!), fight every other male for dominance, and pee all over everything in sight. Including me, in the middle of the show ring...

- Spaying is on balance much healthier for a female dog, though spaying after one year of age has better health outcomes than spaying younger.
- For a male dog, surgical neutering is potentially less healthy; non-surgical neutering is a good option.
- Unlike humans, dogs do not possess 'sexuality'; they will not be emotionally disturbed by neutering, and they will not feel that they are 'missing out' on anything.

MISTAKE 31: PREGNANCY, LABOUR AND PUPPIES, OH MY!

Usually, the most contact anyone has with the whole canine reproduction thing is the 'in heat' issue. Female dogs come into season approximately twice a year. They bleed for a week or two, and are fertile for another week or two after that. While they're in heat, they release pheromones that let all the males in the area know that they're receptive—and when I say area, I mean 'entire neighborhood'. And let me assure you: an entire (unneutered) dog can go absolutely stark raving *mad* for a female in season.

In humans, females might be more receptive when they're ovulating, but often they doesn't notice anything—and males are generally oblivious to the whole thing. Dogs, however, couldn't ignore it if you paid them in fresh beef.

Remember how I said smell is the most important sense to them? Yeah. A dog can't *help* but smell when a female is in season, even if she's a few blocks away, and some dogs will do anything it takes to get that girl. Think broken fences, tunnels in the garden, chewed up restraints, generally berserker attitudes, total incapability to listen to their human or concentrate in any way at all… Of course, not every dog gets it this bad. But the potential remains.

On the other hand, the whole pregnancy/birth/

raising-babies thing is so much less complicated when you're not a human. Dogs gestate for about 63 days; the labor can take over 50 hours. That might sound pretty horrible (the 50 hours—a two month gestation time sounds pretty good to me!), but although it's tiring for the dog, it's not anywhere near as painful as it is for a human mother giving birth. Because there are a lot of puppies—my husband's uncle had a dog who once had *nineteen* puppies in a single litter—they are much smaller proportionately than human babies, so they pop out rather more easily.

If you're interested in all the gory detail, I suggest you visit Lab Tails at http://labtails.blogspot.com, a blog run by a writer and Labrador owner. Trawl through her archives and you'll find several documented litters, including videos of the deliveries and the puppies' subsequent development; September 2008 is particularly helpful.

As for puppies, they're born both blind and deaf. Their ears open at about ten days, and their eyes at about ten to fourteen days. They don't start to vocalize until about two weeks, and then it's mostly whining and whimpering. Real barking doesn't usually start until about two months, and they are fully weaned just before this at about six weeks. The longer a pup is left with its mother, the more well-mannered it will be (especially in canine terms), but eight or nine weeks is usually seen as the minimum age for a pup to be re-homed.

And one final thing—a lot of people think of having a litter of puppies as a quick way to make money. Like all things, if you cut corners, it can be—but to do it well takes time, knowledge and money. Read the Lab Tails blog for October/November 2008 to see just how much money it can take if you're committed to raising a litter of healthy, intelligent, well-developed puppies.

- A bitch in season can wreak havoc on the neighborhood, and any entire dogs within smelling range will do whatever they can to get to her.
- Like most mammals, labor and birth is a fairly private affair, and will often occur in the wee hours of the morning, somewhere the bitch has decided is secluded enough.

MISTAKE 32: ALLERGIES, FUR, AND OTHER REASONS WHY YOU SHOULDN'T HAVE A DOG

The reasons a person gives for *not* having a dog are many and variety, and provide just as much insight into their character as another person's reasons for having a dog. Here are some of the common excuses:

But I can't have a dog! I'm allergic!

Yes, true, people can be allergic to dogs, some even desperately so. This is usually a case of allergies to either the coat (actually the 'dander', the flakes of skin etc. that come off rather than the hair itself) or the saliva—and there are ways around both of these!

If the allergy is to the coat, then it's useful to be aware of so-called 'hypoallergenic' dogs, breed specifically to have coats less likely to induce allergies. The majority of research into 'hypoallergenic' animals has found that there are really too many variables at play to be able to conclude definitively that one breed or another is actually hypoallergenic; however, many people do demonstrate a higher tolerance for some breeds over others. Of course, it varies from person to person and dog to dog—because the actual allergy is to proteins the dog produces, and no two dogs produce the same amount, even with two dogs that are the same breed, one can induce allergies and the other not.

Breeds that have hypoallergenic potential include the Chinese Crested dog (mostly hairless); Poodles and the variations thereon (Cockapoo, Labradoodle, Miniature, Standard, Snoodle, etc); and many terriers, such as the Airdale, Bedlington, Border, Cairn, Kerry Blue, Tibetan, West Highland White, Wire-haired Fox, and the Yorkshire. In general, it's thought that smaller dogs are less allergenic than larger dogs. They have a small surface area from which to shed dander, and are much easier to bath regularly; some studies suggest that bathing a dog twice a week can be enough to minimize or even eliminate an allergic reaction.

If the allergy is to the saliva, oftentimes (though not always) the allergy is actually a reaction to something the dog is eating. Our very first litter of Labrador puppies was raised on a top-quality, premium dog food, one that had given us very good results in the past. However, one puppy from that litter was placed in a home with a young boy who had quite severe egg allergies. It wasn't until he began reacting to his new puppy's saliva and we investigated further that we realized the food we'd been feeding had a significant amount of egg in it. The new owners switched the brand of food to something egg-free, and the son no longer reacted to the puppy's saliva.

But dog fur goes everywhere! If I'm going to get a dog, I should at least get a short-haired breed to prevent this, right?

Uh, no. It's counterintuitive until you think about it,

but long hair is actually a *lot* easier to remove than short dog hair. Short hair is spikey and tends to grab into the fabric of clothes and soft furnishings much more easily than long dog hair. Long hair sticks superficially, but can't work its way into the actual weave of cloth. Short hair is like little tiny needles, and never comes out of the fabric altogether. My husband and I joke that our first Labrador came on our around-the-world trip, because even though we were halfway across the world with freshly laundered clothes, we still had Laura-hair all over us.

But if I get a dog, I'll never be able to go on holidays again!

True and false. True if you have a dog that can't or won't self-regulate its food intake and lack friends or neighbors willing to do a daily food-and-water check. But many holiday destinations these days have accommodation that will gladly cater to canine companions, and it's easier than ever these days to travel with your dog.

Our dogs, used as they are to dog shows and being crated at night, are especially easy to travel with; they sleep for hours on the back seat of the car, toilet mostly on command, and are happy anywhere as long as they are in their portable crates (and there are no strange noises. We won't discuss the first time Max heard wind moaning through cracks in a garage all night long).

But dogs are gross! I don't want an animal that is out licking who-knows-what and then comes in and tries to lick me!

Yeah, okay, I'm pretty much with you on this one. The

good news is, though, that dog saliva is at least mildly antiseptic, acting as a bactericide against both E. coli and Streptococcus.

- Dogs come in hypoallergenic varieties.
- Short dog fur sticks worse than long dog fur.
- Travelling with dogs is easier than ever, with a wide variety of dog-friendly accommodation available.
- Dog saliva might be gross, but at least it's antiseptic against common strains of bacteria.

CONCLUSION

Thank you for reading *The 33 Worst Mistakes Writers Make About Dogs*. I hope that, at least in some small way, I have been able to broaden your understanding of what it is to be a dog, and how canines experience the world. I hope that, even if your work was devoid of dogs before, this book will have given you both a good excuse to introduce some dogs into your stories, and the knowledge of how to do so.

Following is a short list of the resources I've found particularly helpful, both in my research for this book and throughout years of general dog ownership.

Please feel free to contact me either via my blog at http://www.amylaurens.com, or by email at amyllaurens@gmail.com. Remember, there are a whole host of extras specifically designed to accompany this book at http://www.amylaurens.com/books/dog-book.

USEFUL RESOURCES

Lab Tails—http://labtails.blogspot.com—Observations about and lessons learned from a life lived with FIVE fabulous Labrador Retrievers.

Firefly Clicker Training—http://sue-eh.ca/—This site, by Sue Ailsby, has a detailed discussion of the concept of clicker training, along with schedules, exercises, and training programs to get your dog all the way from newborn to extraordinaire.

For The Love Of A Dog: Understanding Emotion In You And Your Best Friend, by Patricia McConnell. An astounding book that combines scientific research with personal anecdotes into a very easy-to-read discussion on the concept of emotion.

Cesar Millan—http://www.cesarmillaninc.com—A great website by one of America's most famous 'dog whisperers'

The Intelligence of Dogs, by Stanley Coren. A unique take on the idea of intelligence as it applies to both dogs and humans.

REFERENCES

SECTION ONE

Best, Ben (2004). *The Amygdala and the Emotions.* http://www.benbest.com/science/anatmind/anatmd9.html [accessed 10 October 2011].

Coren, Stanley (1995). *The Intelligence of Dogs: A Guide to the Thoughts, Emotions and Inner Lives of Our Canine Companions.* Bantam Books.

Dixon, Beth (2001). "Animal Emotions." *Ethics and the Environment* 6(2):22-30.

Gosling, S., Kwan, V. and John, O. (2003). "A Dog's Got Personality: A Cross-Species Comparative Approach to Personality Judgments in Dogs and Humans." *Journal of Personality and Social Psychology* 85(6):1161-9.

Jacks, Beth & Womer, Kelly (2008). *Every Day Thoughts: Words to Woof By.* New Seasons.

Karten, Harvey J. (1997). "Evolutionary Developmental Biology Meets the Brain: The Origins of Mammalian Cortex". *Proceedings of the National Academy of Sciences* 94(7):2800-4.

Lund, J.D., Agger, J.F. & Vestergaard K.S. (1996). "Reported Behaviour Problems in Pet Dogs in Denmark:

Age Distribution and Influence of Breed and Gender." *Preventative Veterinary Medicine* 28:33-48.

McConnell, Patricia (2007). *For The Love Of A Dog: Understanding Emotion In You And Your Best Friend.* Ballantine Books.

Northcutt, R.G. (2002). "Understanding Vertebrate Brain Evolution." *Integrative and Comparative Biology* 42(4):743-56.

O'Keefe, J. & Nadel, L. (1978). *The Hippocampus as a Cognitive Map.* Oxford University Press.

Semendeferi, K., Lu, A., GoVredi, S.K., Schenker, N. & Damasio, H. (2002). "Humans and Great Apes Share a Large Frontal Cortex." *Nature Neuroscience* 5(3):272-6.

Squire, L.R. & Schacter, D.L. (2002). *The Neuropsychology of Memory.* Guilford Press.

Udell, Monique & Wynne, C.D.L (2008). "A Review of Domestic Dogs' (*Canis Familiaris*) Human-Like Behaviors: Or Why Behavior Analysts Should Stop Worrying And Love Their Dogs." *Journal of the Experimental Analysis of Behavior* 89(2):247-61.

SECTION TWO

Bradshaw, J.W.S. (2006). "The Evolutionary Basis for the Feeding Behavior of Domestic Dogs (*Canis Familiaris*) and Cats (*Felis Catus*)." *Journal of Nutrition (Supplement: The WALTHAM International Sciences Symposia Innovations in Companion Animal Nutrition: Nutritional Evolution)* 136:1927S-31S.

Coren, Stanley (2004). *How Dogs Think.* First Free Press, Simon and Schuster.

Elert, Glenn and Condon, Timothy (2003). "Frequency Range of Dog Hearing." *The Physics Factbook.* http://hypertextbook.com/facts/2003/TimCondon.shtml [Accessed 28 September 2011].

Gwaltney-Brant, Sharon (2001). "Chocolate Intoxication." *Veterinary Medicine.* http://www.aspcapro.org/mydocuments/m-toxbrief_0201.pdf [Accessed 28 September 2011].

Meadows, Irina (2006). "Toxicology Brief: The 10 Most Common Toxicoses in Dogs." *Veterinary Medicine* 101(3):142-9.

Miller, P.E. & Murphy, C.J. (1995). "Vision in Dogs". *Journal of American Veterinary Medical Association* 207(12):1623-34.

Neitz, J., Geist, T. & Jacobs, G.H. (1989). "Color Vision in the Dog". *Visual Neuroscience* 3:119-125.

Rathore, A.K. (1984). "Evaluation of Lithium Chloride Taste Aversion in Penned Domestic Dogs." *Journal of Wildlife Management* 48:1424.

Sheldrake, Rupert (2000). *Dogs That Know When Their Owners Are Coming Home: And Other Unexplained Powers of Animals.* Three Rivers Press.

Sueda, K.L.C., et al. (2008). "Characterisation of plant eating in dogs." *Applied Animal Behavior Science* 11(1-2):120-132.

Willis, C.M. *et al.* (2004). "Olfactory Detection of Human Bladder Cancer by Dogs: Proof of Principle Study." *British Medical Journal* 329:712.

SECTION THREE

Coren, Stanley (1995). *The Intelligence of Dogs: A Guide to the Thoughts, Emotions and Inner Lives of Our Canine Companions*. Bantam Books.

Giedd, Jay N. et al. (1999). "Brain Development during childhood and adolescence: a longitudinal MRI study." *Nature Neuroscience* 2(10):861–863.

Lindberg, J. et al. (2005). "Selection for tameness has changed brain gene expression in silver foxes." *Current Biology* 15(22):R915–6.

Morey, Darcy F. (1994). "The Early Evolution of the Domestic Dog." *American Scientist* 82:336-47.

Overmier, J.B. & Seligman, M.E.P. (1967). "Effects of inescapable shock upon subsequent escape and avoidance responding." *Journal of Comparative and Physiological Psychology*. 63:28–33.

Pfungst, O. (1911). *Clever Hans (The horse of Mr. von Osten): A contribution to experimental animal and human psychology* (Trans. C. L. Rahn). New York: Henry Holt.

Serpell, James (1995). *The Domestic Dog; its evolution, behaviour and interactions with people*. Cambridge: Cambridge Univ. Press, p 35.

Sloan, Monty (2012). "Are wolves and wolfdog hybrids trainable?" *Wolf Park*. http://web.archive.org/web/20080615124627/http:/www.wolfpark.org/wolfdogs/Poster_section7.html [Accessed January 7 2012].

Trut, Lyudmila (1999). "Early Canid Domestication: The Farm-Fox Experiment." *American Scientist* 87(2):160.

SECTION FOUR

Alleyne, Richard (October 2008). "Dogs can read emotion in human faces." *Daily Telegraph.* http://www.telegraph.co.uk/science/science-news/3354028/Dogs-can-read-emotion-in-human-faces.html [Accessed 4 October 2011].

Engleberg,Isa N. (2006) "Working in Groups: Communication Principles and Strategies". *My Communication Kit Series*, p133.

SECTION FIVE

Coren, Stanley (1995). *The Intelligence of Dogs: A Guide to the Thoughts, Emotions and Inner Lives of Our Canine Companions.* Bantam Books.

Grady, Denise (5 February 1997). "Nonallergenic Dog? Not Really." *The New York Times.* http://www.nytimes.com/1997/02/05/us/nonallergenic-dog-not-really.html [Accessed 18 October 2011].

Hart, B.L. and Powell, K.L. (1990). "Antibacterial properties of saliva: role in maternal periparturient grooming and in licking wounds." *Physiological Behavior* 48(3):38.

Heutelbeck, A.R.R., Schulz, T., Bergmann, K-C. and Hallier, E. (2008). "Environmental Exposure to Allergens of Different Dog Breeds and Relevance in Allergological Diagnostics." *Journal of Toxicology and Environmental Health, Part A* 71(11):751–8.

Hodson, T., Custovic, A., Simpson, A., Chapman, M., Woodcock, A. and Green, R. (1999). "Washing the dog reduces dog allergen levels, but the dog needs to be washed twice a week." *The Journal of Allergy and Clinical Immunology* 103(4):581–5.

McGreevy, P.D., Thomson, P.C., Pride, C., Fawcett, A., Grassi, T., Jones, B. (May 2005). "Prevalence of obesity in dogs examined by Australian veterinary practices and the risk factors involved." *The Veterinary Record* 156(22):695–702.

Sanborn, Laura J. (2007). "Long-Term Health Risks and Benefits Associated with Spay/Neuter in Dogs." *National Animal Interest Alliance.* http://www.naiaonline.org/pdfs/LongTermHealthEffectsOfSpayNeuterInDogs.pdf [Accessed 2 March 2012]

Savant-Harris, Myra (2006). *Canine Reproduction and Whelping: A Dog Breeder's Guide.* Dogwise Publishing.

Spain, C. Victor, Scarlett, Janet M., Houpt, Katherine A. (2004). "Long-term Risks and Benefits of Early-Age Gonadectomy in Dogs." *Journal of the American Veterinary Medical Association* 224(3):380-7.

Swaminathan, Nikhil. (2008) "Why are different breeds of dogs all considered the same species?" *Scientific* American. http://www.sciam.com/article.cfm?id=different-dog-breeds-same-species [Accessed 20 July 2010].

ABOUT THE AUTHOR

Amy Laurens is a high-school English teacher who usually writes various incarnations of the fantasy genre. She has lived with dogs all her life, and can't possibly imagine a world without impossible-to-eradicate dog fur—er, that is to say, unconditional love and companionship. Her experiences with dogs are wide and varied, and include obedience trials, conformation showing, breeding and more.

You can contact Amy at amyllaurens@gmail.com, or visit her website, www.amylaurens.com.

For bonus extras related to this book, (including videos, images and further commentary), go to:

http://www.amylaurens.com/books/dog-book

www.ingramcontent.com/pod-product-compliance
Lightning Source LLC
Chambersburg PA
CBHW021118080526
44587CB00010B/559